First World War
and Army of Occupation
War Diary
France, Belgium and Germany

4 CAVALRY DIVISION
Divisional Troops
Brigade Ammunition Column
1 January 1917 - 31 December 1917

WO95/1158/3

The Naval & Military Press Ltd
www.nmarchive.com
Published in association with The National Archives

Published by

The Naval & Military Press Ltd

Unit 10 Ridgewood Industrial Park,

Uckfield, East Sussex,

TN22 5QE England

Tel: +44 (0) 1825 749494

www.naval-military-press.com

www.nmarchive.com

This diary has been reprinted in facsimile from the original. Any imperfections are inevitably reproduced and the quality may fall short of modern type and cartographic standards.

© Crown Copyright
Images reproduced by permission of The National Archives, London, England, 2015.

Contents

Document type	Place/Title	Date From	Date To
Heading	WO95/1158/3		
Heading	B C F 4 Cav. Div. 16 Bde R.H.A. Ammo Col 1917 Jan To 1917 Dec		
Heading	War Diary of 4th Cavalry Divisional Ammunition Column. From 1st January 1917 To 31st January 1917.		
War Diary		01/01/1917	31/12/1917

WO 95/1158/3

BEF
4 Cav. Div.
16 Bde RHA Ammo Col

1917 Jan — 1917 Dec

SERIAL NO. 283

Confidential
War Diary
of

4TH CAVALRY DIVISIONAL AMMUNITION COLUMN.

FROM 1st JANUARY 1917 TO 31st JANUARY 1917.

Army Form C. 2118.

Confidential

WAR DIARY
or
INTELLIGENCE SUMMARY.
(Erase heading not required.)

JANUARY 1917

Place	Date	Hour	Summary of Events and Information	Remarks and references to Appendices
January	1st to 31st 1917		Remained at FRESSENNEVILLE during the Month	

Signed,
COMMDG. 4th CAVALRY DIVN. AMMN. COL.

Army Form C. 2118.

WAR DIARY
INTELLIGENCE SUMMARY.
(Erase heading not required.)

FEBRUARY 1917

Instructions regarding War Diaries and Intelligence Summaries are contained in F. S. Regs., Part II. and the Staff Manual respectively. Title pages will be prepared in manuscript.

Place	Date	Hour	Summary of Events and Information	Remarks and references to Appendices
	1st February		Still at FRESSENNEVILLE	
	26th	8.15 A.M.	B Sub Sec and C Sub sec of the 2nd Section left FRESSENNEVILLE and marched with "A" Battery R.H.A. and proceeded to BECORDEL	
	2nd to 25th Feb.		Remained at FRESSENNEVILLE	

CAPT. R.H.A.
COMMDG. 4th CAVALRY DIVN. AMMN. COL

Army Form C. 2118.

WAR DIARY

INTELLIGENCE SUMMARY

(Erase heading not required.)

MARCH 1917.

Place	Date	Hour	Summary of Events and Information	Remarks and references to Appendices
	1st to 18th March		Remained at FRESSENNEVILLE	HAT
	19th		Left FRESSENNEVILLE 10.0 A.M. and proceeded by march route to NEUF MOULIN arriving at 2. P.M.	HAT
	20th		Left NEUF MOULIN 10.30 AM and proceeded by march route to FIEFFE arriving at 3.30 pm	HAT
	21st		Left FIEFFE 11.15 A.M. and proceeded by march route to ALBERT arriving at 11.0 P.M.	HAT
	22nd to 26th		Remained at ALBERT.	HAT
	27th	9.45 AM	Left ALBERT and proceeded by march route to BOIS DE LOGEAST arriving at 3. P.M. and joined up with B & C Sub-Sects. of the 2nd Section	HAT
	28th to 31st		Remained at BOIS DE LOGEAST.	HAT

Army Form C. 2118.

WAR DIARY
of
INTELLIGENCE SUMMARY.
(Erase heading not required.)

APRIL 1917

Instructions regarding War Diaries and Intelligence Summaries are contained in F. S. Regs., Part II. and the Staff Manual respectively. Title pages will be prepared in manuscript.

Place	Date	Hour	Summary of Events and Information	Remarks and references to Appendices
	1st to 9th April		Remained at BOIS DE LOGEAST.	XXT
	10th		Left BOIS DE LOGEAST 6.30 AM and proceeded by march route to ERVILLERS. On arriving at COURCELLES received orders to return to camp just vacated.	XXX
	11th to 30th		Remained at BOIS DE LOGEAST.	XXX

WAR DIARY Ammn Col. 16th Bde R.H.A.
of
INTELLIGENCE SUMMARY.
(Erase heading not required.)

Army Form C. 2118.

MAY 1917.

Place	Date	Hour	Summary of Events and Information	Remarks and references to Appendices
	1st to 9th May		Remained at Bois de Loge East.	AAA
	10th May		Left Bois de Loge East 2 p.m. and proceeded by march route to Le Transloy arriving at 5 p.m.	AAA
	11th		Remained at Le Transloy	AAA
	12th		Left Le Transloy 10 a.m. and proceeded by march route to Moislans arriving at 2 p.m.	AAA
	13th		Left Moislans 12.30 A.M. and proceeded by march route to Bouchy arriving at 3 p.m.	AAA
	14th		Left Bouchy 3.45 p.m. and proceeded by march route to Tertry arriving at 5 p.m.	AAA
	15th to 22nd		Remained at Tertry	AAA
	23rd		Left Tertry 1.30 p.m. and proceeded by march route to Bouchy arriving at 3 p.m.	AAA
	24th to 31st		Remained at Bouchy.	AAA

CAPT. R.H.A.
COMDG. 4th CAVALRY DIVN. AMMN. COL.

Army Form C. 2118.

June 1917.

WAR DIARY
or
INTELLIGENCE SUMMARY.
(Erase heading not required.)

Place	Date	Hour	Summary of Events and Information	Remarks and references to Appendices
1st to 13th June			Remained at BOUCLY	XXT
14th			Left BOUCLY 11 a.m. & proceeded by march route to HANCOURT arriving at 11.45 a.m.	XXT
15th to 30th June			Remained at HANCOURT.	XXT

COMMDG. 4th CAVALRY DIVN. AMMN. COL.
CAPT. R.H.A.

Army Form C. 2118.

Dist Ammn Column
4th Cav Div July 1917

WAR DIARY
or
INTELLIGENCE SUMMARY.
(Erase heading not required.)

Instructions regarding War Diaries and Intelligence Summaries are contained in F.S. Regs., Part II. and the Staff Manual respectively. Title pages will be prepared in manuscript.

Place	Date	Hour	Summary of Events and Information	Remarks and references to Appendices
	1st to 23rd July		Remained at HANCOURT	WAT
	24th "		Left HANCOURT 10.45 A.M. & proceeded by march route to ATHIES arriving at 11.30 A.M.	WAT
	25th to 31st "		Remained at ATHIES	WAT

[signature]
CAPT. R.H.A.
COMMDG. 4th CAVALRY DIVN. AMMN. COL.

Army Form C. 2118.

24

WAR DIARY
or
INTELLIGENCE SUMMARY.
(Erase heading not required.)

August 1917

Place	Date	Hour	Summary of Events and Information	Remarks and references to Appendices
	1st to 31st Aug.		Remained at ATHIES.	

COMMDG. 4th CAVALRY DIVN. AMMN. COL. R.H.A.

WAR DIARY of 4th Cav. Div. Amm. Column. Army Form C. 2118.

INTELLIGENCE SUMMARY. September 1917. Serial No. 283

(Erase heading not required.)

Place	Date	Hour	Summary of Events and Information	Remarks and references to Appendices
1st to 30th Sept.			Remained at ATHIES	Nil

[signature]
Capt. R.H.A.
COMMDG. 4th CAVALRY DIVN. AMMN. COL.

4th Cav. Fd. Ammn Column

Army Form C. 2118.

283

WAR DIARY

INTELLIGENCE SUMMARY
(Erase heading not required.)

OCTOBER 1917.

Place	Date	Hour	Summary of Events and Information	Remarks and references to Appendices
	1st to 31st Oct 1917		Remained at ATHIES	NIL

J.B. Ingle
CAPT. R.H.A.
COMMDG. 4th CAVALRY DIVN. AMMN. COL.

Army Form C. 2118.

283

WAR DIARY
or
INTELLIGENCE SUMMARY.
(Erase heading not required.)

4th Cav¥. Ammn Column
November 1917

Place	Date	Hour	Summary of Events and Information	Remarks and references to Appendices
	1st to 13 Nov 1917		Remained at ATHIES.	
	14th	4.30 PM	Left ATHIES 4.30 PM and proceeded by march route to VAUX WOOD arriving there 10.30 PM	
	15th to 18th		Remained at VAUX WOOD	
	19th	6.30 PM	Left VAUX WOOD 6.30 PM and proceeded by march route to QUEENS CROSS arriving there 11.30 PM	
	20th	2.30 PM	Left QUEENS CROSS 2.30 PM " " " " BEAUCAMP " 5.30 PM	
		9.30 PM	Left BEAUCAMP 9.30 PM " " " " VILLERS PLOUICH " 10.0 PM	
	21st	8.30 AM	Left VILLERS PLOUICH 8.30 AM " " " " BEAUCAMP " 11.0 AM	
	22nd to 28th		Remained at BEAUCAMP	
	29th	9.30 AM	Left BEAUCAMP 9.30 AM " " " " ATHIES " 5.0 PM	
	30th	1.0 PM	Left ATHIES 1.0 PM " " " " LONGAVESNES " 7.30 PM	

[signature]
CAPT. R.H.A.
COMMDG. 4th CAVALRY DIVN. AMMN. COL.

Army Form C. 2118.

4th Cavalry Amm Column

(283)

December 1917

WAR DIARY
or
INTELLIGENCE SUMMARY.
(Erase heading not required.)

Place	Date	Hour	Summary of Events and Information.	Remarks and references to Appendices
1st Dec 17			Left LONGAVESNES 6.30 AM and proceeded by march route to SAULCOURT arriving there 7.30 AM	A.O.t
2 to 6th			Remained at SAULCOURT	A.O.t
7th			Left SAULCOURT 9.30 am and proceeded by march route to ATHIES arriving there 1.40 p.m.	A.O.t
8 to 31st			Remained at ATHIES.	A.O.t

A.C. Smith. Lt. R.F.A.
Adjt.
4th R.H.A.
COMMDG. 4th CAVALRY DVN. AMMN. COL.

www.ingramcontent.com/pod-product-compliance
Lightning Source LLC
Chambersburg PA
CBHW081253170426
43191CB00037B/2141